THE SEARCH FOR SPACE IN FOOTBALL

26 TRAINING SESSIONS FOR THE CREATION OF SPACE

MATTEO VON DER HORST

The search for space in football / Matteo Von Der Horst. - 1st ed.
LIBROFUTBOL.com, 2022.

110 pages; 15,2 x 22,9 cm.

ISBN 978-987-8943-28-2

1. Football
CDD 796.334

THE SEARCH FOR SPACE IN FOOTBALL
by Matteo Von Der Horst

Cover design: Luciano Medvetkin Authors photo: Matteo Von Der Horst	Cover photo: © Paul Terry / Sportage Credit: Sportage / Alamy Live News
© 2022 – Matteo Von Der Horst © 2022 – LIBROFUTBOL.com	All rights reserved

ISBN 978-987-8943-28-2 | 1st edition: September 2022

ediciones@librofutbol.com

+54 9 11 2215 1982

librofutbol

Av. del Libertador 6898 – City of Buenos Aires – Argentina

INDEX

INTRODUCTION

Football games are becoming more and more similar to chess matches, where two very tactically organized sides battle it out. This trend indicates that the majority of coaches have the objective to defend, due to the fear of conceding a goal, against the possibility of taking on the risk of attacking to try and score in the opposition's net.

Many are confused that modern football only consists of passing the ball from one side to another, however it is necessary to interpret every situation to be able to provide a significant purpose to the possession of the ball. One objective that helps us achieve the goal of our side: slow the tempo of the game and rest physically, tire out and panic the opponents, suck the adversary into a certain area on the field to later attack another when they least expect it.

To be able to transmit to our team these necesarry objectives that allow us to carry out proper possession of the ball, we need to have clear the sequence of exercises appropriate to our style of play.

This series of exercises has been divided into two parts: the first involves the individual concepts to create space, while the second will incorporate the concepts related to the collaboration and work as a team.

The proposed ideas here come from experiences taken in direct form from personal training sessions of the author and exchanged ideas with other coaches. Upon finishing the book you will be able to adapt these exercises to your own team, according to the objectives that you wish to achieve.

CHAPTER 1
CONTINUOUS MOVEMENT

12 - DRILLS TO LOSE MARKERS AND THE OPEN PASSING LANE

The first step to creating space is to move: I understand movement as something that always has a purpose, dynamism and contextualized to the sport in question. In football it is very important to work on body shape in line with the movement of the ball, orientating it towards the direction where one wants to carry out the move. It is even more important to know how to visualize the available space and understand how to move.

In some cases the speed of the player does not matter: Xavi and Pirlo, for example, are two players thinking about constant movement that do not have a quick change of pace, so they have to always be in the correct spot at the correct time.

The best way to work on this concept is to make the players understand the importance of being unmarked. In other words, free yourself from the marking by the defender. To receive the ball it is necessary to leave the area of the opposition's influence. This is a concept that

we discount, but it often happens that we listen to managers suggest to their players that they move more, or seeing the typical player at a stand-still on the field, complaining that they are not receiving the ball while they are clearly being marked.

In football, to create an "open passing lane" means that in the passing lanes there is no opponent between the player who has the ball and the one who is going to receive it. It involves a fundamental basis to be able to have a solid possession of the ball. The more players of the same team that go unmarked, the more solutions there will be for a player with the ball, who can pick and choose their options. The best teams in the world use their multiple passing options as a way of creating superior numbers.

OPEN PASSING LANE

01

HOW IT'S DONE

HOW IT'S DONE

Simplified situation

DURATION

10 minutes

OBJECTIVES

- **Lose marker**
- **Receive**
- **Pass**
- **Mobility**
  or movement

MATERIALS

- **4 cones**
- **Balls**

PREPARATION

- **Area of play: 10×10 meters**
- **Players: 4**
- **Number of sets: 4 of 2 minutes with 30 second breaks in between the sets**

ORGANIZATION

In a square of 10×10 meters put a cone in the center of each side. Player A starts from one cone with the ball, at the opposite cone players C and D set up and in the middle of the square, on the same line, opponent B sets themself up.

DESCRIPTION

- Players A, C and D play together, while B trys to intercept in the passing lanes.
- C sprints diagonally towards the cone of their choice and D sprints towards the opposite one.
- B closes one passing lane and A passes the ball to the open teammate between C and D. The middle player is substituted each set.

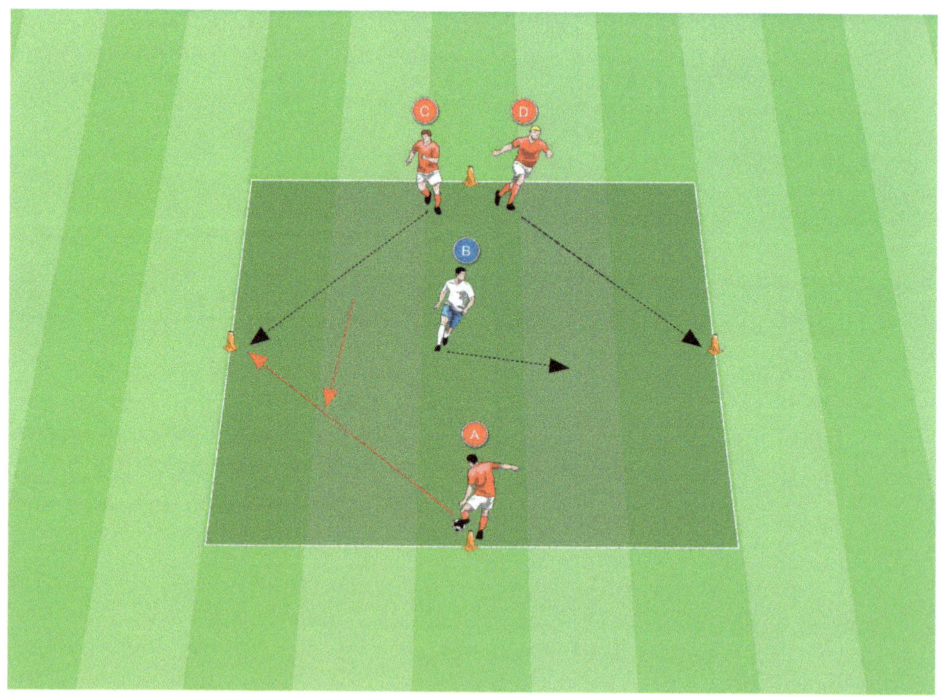

VARIATIONS

1. Put a goal on the opposite point to A to finish off the move with a 3 on 1.

TRAINER'S TIPS

- C carries out the first move, to try and create a passing lane with A.
- B has to stay in a spot that allows them to see A and C.
- Once the passing lane between A and C is occupied by B, D will make a move to create another.
- The moves have to be carried out with maximum intensity because A will not have much time to think in a situation with even numbers.

BALL POSSESSION 2 ON 1 IN PINNIES

02

| HOW IT'S DONE | Simplified situation |

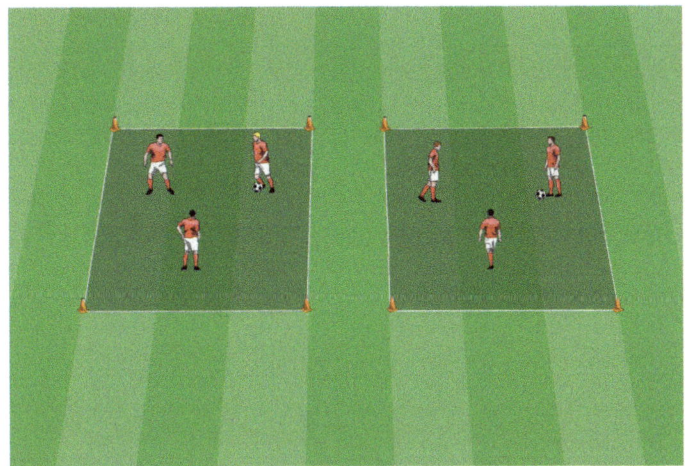

DURATION

12 minutes

OBJECTIVES

- Lose marker
- Pass
- Interception
- Contrast
- 2 on 1

MATERIALS

- 8 cones
- Balls

PREPARATION

- Area of play: 10×20 meters
- Players: 6
- Number of sets: 2 of 5 minutes with 1 minute of rest between sets

ORGANIZATION

Create two mirrored squares of 8×8 meters. A 2 on 1 is played in the middle, all players are without pinnies.

DESCRIPTION

- In two mirrored squares a 2 on 1 without pinnies is played.
- At the start of the drill the coach decides who starts as the defender, while the other two players in continuous movement have to try to maintain possession
- If the defender intercepts the ball, the last one becomes an attacker and whoever lost possession of the ball becomes the defender.
- After each minute the coach blows the whistle and the players change squares at top speed to restart the drill in the other square.

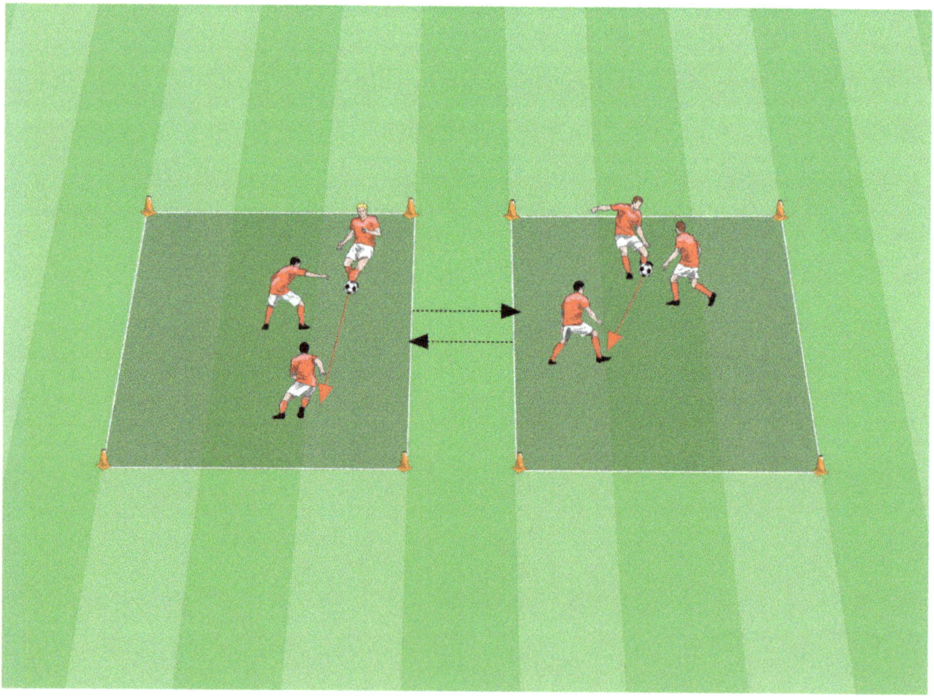

RULES

- The players start the drill with unlimited touches, to later switch to three touches and finally two touches.

TRAINER'S TIPS

- The two players that start with the ball, to be able to receive and pass, have to always be in the open passing lane or lose their marker behind the defender who is pressing.
- The drill, on top of working on losing a marker, serves to teach the players in possession, that after losing the ball it is necessary to do everything possible to win it back again.

BALL POSSESSION 5 ON 5 CONDITIONING

03

| HOW IT'S DONE | Simplified situation |

DURATION

15 minutes

OBJECTIVES

- Lose marker
- Marking
- Interception
- Mobility or movement
- Ball possession

MATERIALS

- 4 cones
- 5 pinnies
- Balls

PREPARATION

- Area of play: 20×30 meters
- Players: 10
- Number of sets: 3 of 4 minutes with 1 minute of rest between sets

ORGANIZATION

Create a playing field of 20×30 meters with the help of the cones. Within the area a 5 5 is played.

DESCRIPTION

- A 5 on 5 possession of the ball with two touches is played.
- When a player in possession of the ball is touched by the hands of a defender, possession flips to the other team.
- Ten consecutive passes is worth one point.

RULES

- Possession of the ball is played with two touches.
- If a player gets touched by the hands of an opponent, possession flips to the other team.

VARIATIONS

1. It is possible to play out the possession while using hands, but passes have to be carried out below the shoulder.

TRAINER'S TIPS

- The field needs to be very wide at the start, so that play flows and so the team in possession uses the open space.
- Players have to always place themselves in open space on the field, where there are no opponents, to avoid being tagged the moment they come into possession of the ball.
- Once play starts to flow, the field can be reduced to turn up the pace.
- After a pass, get the player in search of a new space on the field to occupy.

MINIGAME 1 ON 1: MAN TO MAN

04

HOW IT'S DONE — Simplified situation

DURATION

15 minutes

OBJECTIVES

- Lose marker
- Marking
- Mobility or movement

MATERIALS

- Cones
- 8 pinnies
- 2 goals
- Balls

PREPARATION

- Area of play: 50×70 meters
- Players: 16 + 2 goalkeepers
- Number of sets: 2 of 6 minutes with 1 minute and 30 second breaks in between sets

ORGANIZATION

Create a 50×70 meter field with the cones and place a goal on both of the shorter sides. An 8 on 8 is played on the field; the goalkeepers cover the goals.

DESCRIPTION

- 8 on 8 game.
- One player on each team marks a specific player of the opposing team no matter the position.
- Starts without a touch limit.
- The team with the most goals wins.

RULES

- Each player must only mark their established opponent before the start of the game.

VARIATIONS

1. Play with a maximum of two or three touches.

TRAINER'S TIPS

- Get the players to move continuously to lose their marker.
- Make the player responsible for marking and not losing their opponent throughout.
- Playing the game with a two or three touch limit developes the principle of the teammates losing their markers.

RONDO 4 ON 1: THREE PASSING LANES

05

| HOW IT'S DONE | Simplified situation |

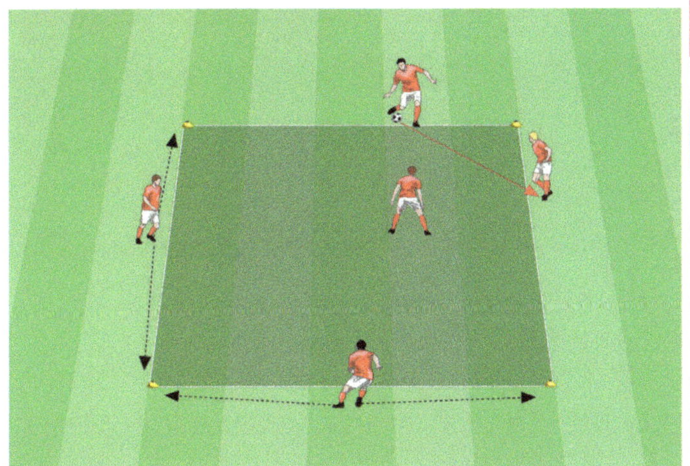

DURATION

10 minutes

OBJECTIVES

- **Ball possession**
- **Interception**
- **Help pass**

MATERIALS

- **4 cones**
- **Balls**

PREPARATION

- **Area of play: 5×5 meters**
- **Players: 5**
- **Number of sets: 2 of 4 minutes with 1 minute of rest between sets**

ORGANIZATION

Create a 5×5 meter square. A player sets up on each side with one opponent on the inside of the square.

DESCRIPTION

- A 4 on 1 rondo is played.
- The objective of the four outside players is trying not to let the opponent who is in the middle of the square intercept the possession.
- The inside player takes the spot of the person on the outside upon intercepting.

RULES

- The rondo is played with a maximum of two touches.
- Ten consecutive passes equal one point.

VARIABLES

1. Give the rondo a one touch limit.

TRAINER'S TIPS

- It is very important that the rondo is played at a fast pace.
- Work on the body shape of the player verifying that they are "open" in the direction of play and teammates.
- The pass must be carried out with the correct intensity.
- Work the time that passes between the control and the pass trying to cut it down.
- The technical execution has to be carried out with a head held high: make the players focus the attention on the play making the handling of the ball automatic.
- Get the players moving and losing their markers according to the positioning of the defender to make advantageous passing lanes.
- Make the player think before the ball arives: in modern football, invisioning the move can change the success of play.
- Try to get the players to carry out the rondo with just one touch.

RONDO 4 ON 2: POINT FOR A PASS BETWEEN DEFENDERS

06

HOW IT'S DONE — Simplified situation

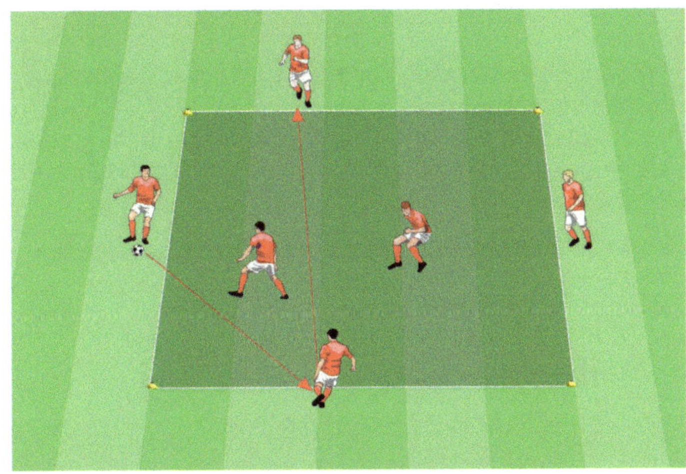

DURATION

10 minutes

OBJECTIVES

- Help pass
- Peripheral vision
- Pass
- Interception

MATERIALS

- 4 cones
- Balls

PREPARATION

- Area of play: 8×8 meters
- Players: 6
- Number of sets: 2 of 4 minutes with 1 minute of rest between sets

ORGANIZATION

Create a square of play of 8×8 meters. Have one player on each side with two opponents on the inside. Create other squares so the entire squad can all play at the same time.

DESCRIPTION

- A 4 on 2 rondo is played.
- The four outside players keep possession and have to pick out the best pass depending on the positioning of the inside opponents.
- 1 point is earned for each pass between the defenders (example in the graphic).
- If one of the two inside players takes the ball they take the position of the player which they stole it from.

RULES

- 1 point is earned for each pass between the defenders.

TRAINER'S TIPS

- It is important that the outside players accustom themselves to find the passing lane as early as possible.
- Limit touches to a maximum of two as a way of elevating the pace to the drill.
- Get the players to move themselves laterally along the square taking up all the width.

RONDO 3 ON 1: OCUPPY THE FREE SPACE

07

HOW IT'S DONE — Simplified situation

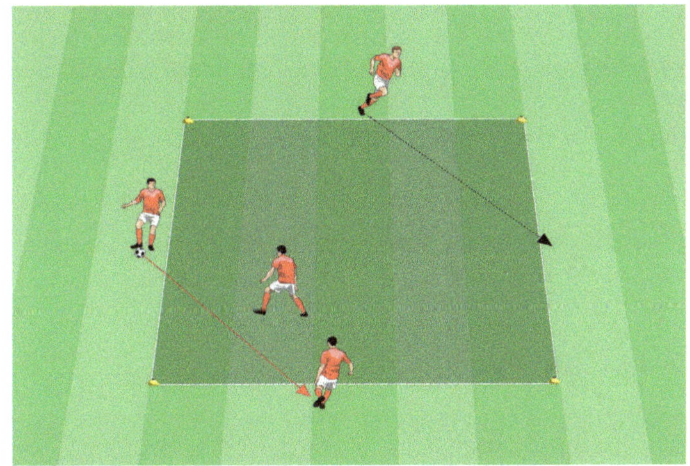

DURATION

10 minutes

OBJECTIVES

- Lose marker
- Pass
- Interception
- Mobility or movement
- Help pass

MATERIALS

- 4 cones
- Balls

PREPARATION

- Area of play: 5×5 meters
- Players: 4
- Number of sets: 2 of 4 minutes with 1 minute of rest between sets

ORGANIZATION

Create a 5×5 meter square. Leave one side open, while on the others one player sets up. Put one opponent in the middle.

DESCRIPTION

- A rondo of 3 on 1 rooted in that the outside player in possession of the ball always has to have two lateral passing options (one teammate to the left and the right); this way the players move to create passing lanes.
- If the inside player gets the ball they take the position of the player who gave the ball away.

RULES

- Play the rondo with a two touch maximum.
- Award 1 point after 10 consecutive passes.

TRAINER'S TIPS

- It is very important for the rondo to be carried out at a high pace.
- Work the body shape of the player verifying that they are "open" towards the direction of play and teammates.
- The pass has to be carried out with the proper intensity.
- Work the time that passes between the control and pass trying to cut it down.
- The technical execution has to be carried out with a head held high: make the players focus the attention on the play making the handling of the ball automatic.
- Make the player think before the ball arives: in modern football invisioning the move can change the success of play.
- Try to get the players to carry out the rondo with just one touch.
- Stimulate the position changes of the players in possession of the ball: ball play and change of position.

PASS AND OCCUPY OPEN SPACE

08

| HOW IT'S DONE | Simplified situation |

DURATION

14 minutes

OBJETIVOS

- Touch and move
- Pass
- Interception

MATERIALS

- 8 cones
- Balls

PREPARATION

- Area of play: 10×10 meters
- Players: 8
- Number of sets: 2 of 6 minutes with 1 minute breaks between sets

ORGANIZATION

Create an octagon placing the cones like in the graphic above. Seven players each set themselves up on a side with one opponent in the middle .

DESCRIPTION

- The seven outside players have to maintain possession without giving it away to the inside opponent.
- Every player who completes a pass must then go to occupy the free side of the octagon.
- The opponent in the middle takes the position of the outside player, should they intercept possession.

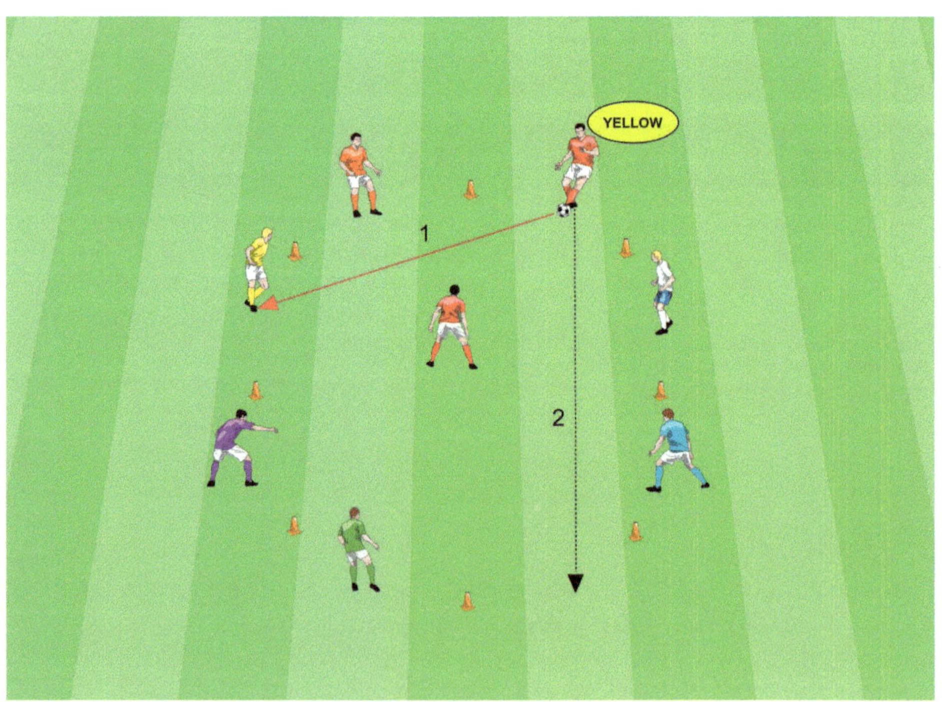

VARIATIONS

1. Play the rondo with a two touch maximum.
2. Give out pinnies of, at the least, three different colors. The players have to call out the color of the pinnie of their intented target before passing.

TRAINER'S TIPS

- Assure a good reaction time in the spot change of the players after having completed a pass.
- Work the peripheral vision of the players so they spot the open position to occupy with anticipation.
- The drill could be very difficult, especially at the beginning. Encourage the players to fire them up at the start.
- Gradually add more difficulty with the calling out of the colors.

4 ON 2: PASSING LANES

09

Simplified situation

DURATION

15 minutes

OBJECTIVES

- **Help pass**
- **2 on 2**
- **Ball possession**
- **Avoid split passes**

MATERIALS

- **8 cones (4 per color)**
- **4 sticks**
- **2 pinnies**
- **Balls**

PREPARATION

- **Area of play: 15×10 meters**
- **Players: 6**
- **Number of sets: 3 of 4 minutes with 1 minute breaks between sets**

ORGANIZATION

Create a rectangle of 15×10 meters and divide it into three parts making the middle part stand out with different colored cones. On both short sides of the rectangle make a two meter goal with the sticks. The two defenders place themselves in the middle zone, while in the other two stand the four players who must maintain possession.

DESCRIPTION

- Rectangle of play is divided into three zones. The middle zone, and smallest, is the interception zone for the two defenders and the other two zones are for the four players who are maintaining possession and creating passing lanes.
- If the two defenders intercept the ball, a 2 on 2 begins with the players that lost possession. The objective of the defenders is to score in the net.
- Once finished, the two players who gave up their possession then move into the middle zone to become the defenders.

RULES

- The outside players keeping possession have only two touches.
- The ball does not need to ever be stopped.
- The players of the same zone Can only pass the ball once between each other. Then they have to move the ball to the opposite zone.

TRAINER'S TIPS

- Get the players of the opposite zone to create passing lanes, losing their markers by moving at the backs of their defenders.
- Have continuous ball movement.
- Players in possession must take into account the width and depth of their zone at hand, making use of the entire playing field.
- The players in the interception zone, to avoid split passes between the two, have to take up a good position through working together.

PASS AND GO TO TEAMMATE'S SPOT

10

HOW IT'S DONE — Simplified situation

DURATION

10 minutes

OBJECTIVES

- Touch and move
- Pass
- Mobility and movement

MATERIALS

- 4 cones
- 1 pinny
- Balls

PREPARATION

- Area of play: 8×8 meters
- Players: 6
- Number of sets: 2 of 4 minutes with 1 minute of rest between sets

ORGANIZATION

Create a playing square of 5×5 meters with the cones with a player on each point. A player starts with the ball on the inside and one opponent with a pinny.

DESCRIPTION

- The five players exchange the ball at the points of the square and after every pass take the former spot of the teammate who they passed the ball to.
- To start the rotation of the outside players at the beginning, one of them has to split the middle zone choosing where to carry out the first pass.
- In the middle of the square is an opponent who tries to take back the ball; they take the spot of the player who gave possession up, should they get it back.

RULES

- The players that exchange the ball play with a one touch maximum.
- The players can only receive the ball at the points of the square.
- The player that carries out the pass has to go to the former spot of the teammate who he passed the ball to.

VARIATIONS

1. Add five pinny colors. The players, before making the passes, have to shout the color of the pinny of the teammate who they are going to pass the ball to.

TRAINER'S TIPS

- The players who have to maintain possession always have one or two passes, in other words the one who freed up the middle opponent.
- Once the ball is played, the players must occupy the free space generated by other teammates, because they are in constant movement.
- Having the opponent in the middle trying to intercept the ball also works peripheral vision.

MOVING IN THE OPEN PASSING LANE

11

DURATION

12 minutes

OBJECTIVES

- Help pass
- Pass
- Interception
- Mobility or movement

MATERIAL

- 8 cones
- 2 pinnies
- Balls

PREPARATION

- Area of play: 10×10 meters
- Players: 6
- Number of sets: 2 of 5 minutes with 1 minute rest in between sets

ORGANIZATION

Create a square of 10×10 meters with the cones. Three players set up on three points with one point staying open. In the middle create another one of 5×5 meters: this smaller square should be rotated to have it's points at the middle of the sides of the outer square. In the space outside the little square and inside the big one should be two opponents in pinnies, with one player on the inside of the little square.

DESCRIPTION

- The three players on the points maintain possession through playing with the player inside the small square trying not to let the two opponents intercept play.
- The three players move themselves between the points to create passing lanes.
- The intercepter takes the position of the passer.
- The player in the small square cannot leave it and has a maximum of two touches.
- The two defenders can only attempt to take away the ball defending their space between the two squares.

TRAINER'S TIPS

- Try to get the players, gradually, to carry out the rondo with one touch.
- The inside player has to move themself trying to create "triangle possessions" with the outside players.
- Encourage movement of position between the players with the possession: touch and move.
- Get the outside players to move according to the inside defenders, in a way that always creates three passing alternatives.
- Staying put without losing their marker has to correspond to a precise tactical move by the player.

BALL POSSESSION: WILD CARD WITH FEWER NUMBERS

12

HOW IT'S DONE — Simplified situation

DURATION

15 minutes

OBJECTIVES

- Lose marker
- Pass
- Mobility or movement
- Ball possession

MATERIALS

- 9 pinnies (6 of one color, 3 of another)
- Balls

PREPARATION

- Area of play: circle with 15 meter diameter
- Players: 14
- Number of sets: 3 of 4 minutes with 1 minute of rest in between sets

ORGANIZATION

Six players with pinnies set up along the perimeter of the circle. Five players set up on the inside without pinnies and three with different colored pinnies that play as wild cards.

DESCRIPTION

- The three wild card players set up in the middle play with the players on the perimteter (red ones in the graphic) while the five play as defenders.
- The outside players on the perimeter have to maintain possession of the ball with the help of the three wild card players who can move freely within the field of play.
- A point is given when all three wild card players touch the ball.

RULES

- The outside players can pass it amongst each other, but only have one touch to do so.
- The point is given after the three wild card players have touched the ball.

TRAINER'S TIPS

- The outside players have to wait for the right moment to be able to pass it to the inside.
- Get the wild card players in the middle of the field to move continuously to have the possibility to get the ball.

CHAPTER 2
THE IMPORTANCE OF LOSING THE MARKER

10 - DRILLS FOR LOSING MARKERS

"We don't have a striker because our striker is the open space", Josep Guardiola

The combined marker loss is a movement that tricks the opponent and is used to attack the opposing space where one wishes to receive the ball. It is an important movement to evade the opponent, but it is necessary to work the timing well or it will be ineffective.

A fundamental difference exists between movement to lose a marker that is carried out to continue ball movement and the movement to lose a marker to attack depth. The first is associated with the search for space to receive a pass between the opposition lines, while the second is related to a movement that has a precise direction (towards goal) on the hunt for depth.

It is not simple to do, not only with timing but also the shape one must take on to not lose sight of the ball. Some strikers use it to attack in

deep receving the ball behind the line of defense: a sure way of causing danger for the opponent. It is a movement that can be done in any area on the field and in different ways: long to short to come in close, short to long to attack depth, in to out for exterior balls, out to in for interior balls. Knowing how to maintain possession will not cut it, it is necesarry to be able to choose the opportune moment to convert it into a dangerous opportunity and attack the depth.

LOSING MARKER FROM OUT TO IN, SWAP AND SHOOT

13

HOW IT'S DONE — Simplified situation

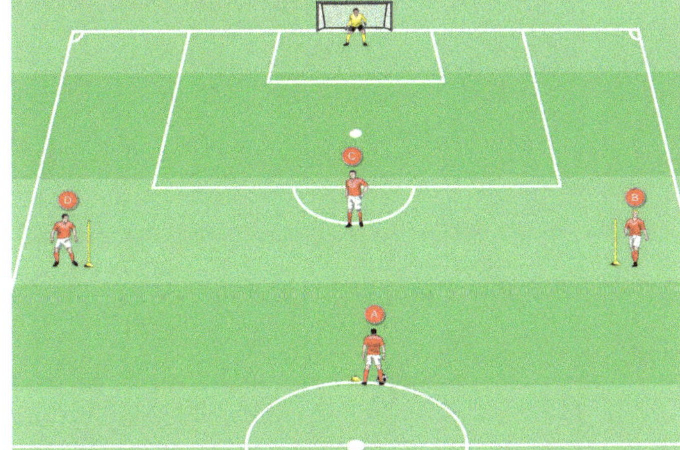

DURATION

10 minutes

OBJECTIVES

- Lose marker in support
- Oriented control
- Pass
- Finish
- Shot on goal

MATERIALS

- 2 posts
- 1 cone
- 1 goal
- Balls

PREPARATION

- Area of play: 50×50 meters
- Players: 8 + 1 goalkeeper
- Number of sets: 2 of 5 minutes

ORGANIZATION

Position two posts in the wide areas of the field of play 10 meters from the area. Put the start cone 35 meters from the goal. Player A starts off to the side of the start cone, while players B and D set up alongside the posts. Player C just outside the area around the half circle. Put two players at each station, the goalkeeper in net.

DESCRIPTION

- B loses their marker firstly opening up to the outside.
- A passes the ball towards B who sets up while anticipating the ball.
- B, after an orientated control, passes the ball to C.
- C, after an orientated control, finishes on goal.
- A will go to the spot of B, B to that of C and C to the position of A. Carry this out down the right side and the left side.

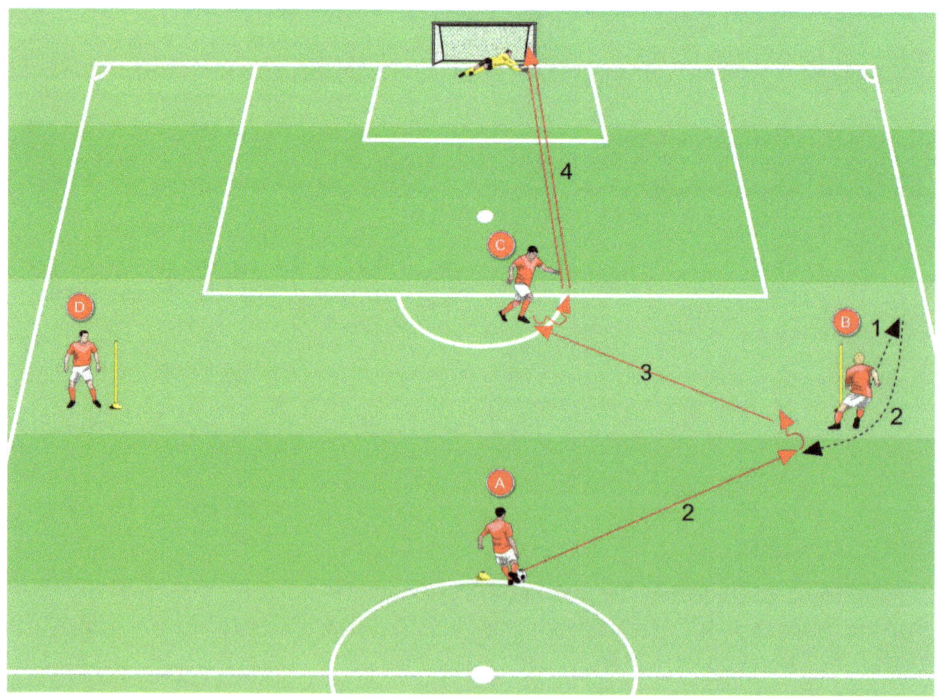

RULES

- The player that loses their marker has two touches at their disposal, an orientated control and a pass.

TRAINER'S TIPS

- Verify the timing of the losing of the marker.
- Verify the orientated control of the outside player who loses their marker in approximation: the first touch determines the success of the play.
- Assure the precision and intensity of the passes.

LOSING MARKER FROM IN TO OUT, ATTACK DEPTH AND STOPPED BALL

14

HOW IT'S DONE — Simplified situation

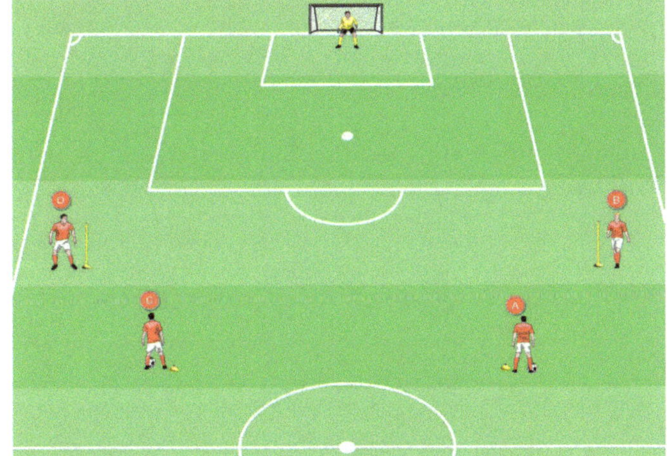

DURATION

15 minutes

OBJECTIVES

- Lose marker in support
- Orientated control
- Pass
- Stopped ball
- Finish
- Shot on goal

MATERIALS

- 2 posts
- Cones
- 1 goal
- Balls

PREPARATION

- Area of play: 50×50 meters
- Players: 12 + 1 goalkeeper
- Number of sets: 3 of 5 minutes

ORGANIZATION

Position the two posts in the wide areas of the field 10 meters from the area. Put the two start cones 35 meters from goal. Players A and C start alongside their cone, while players B and D are alongside their posts. Put three players at each station. The goalkeeper defends the net.

DESCRIPTION

- B loses their marker going towards player A.
- A carries out a long pass to B, attacking the depth.
- B, following an orientated control, hangs the ball up in the air for C who attacks towards the penalty spot.
- C finishes on net.
- Carry out this drill from both the left and the right. The wingers who cross the ball have a maximum of two passes at their disposal (control and pass).

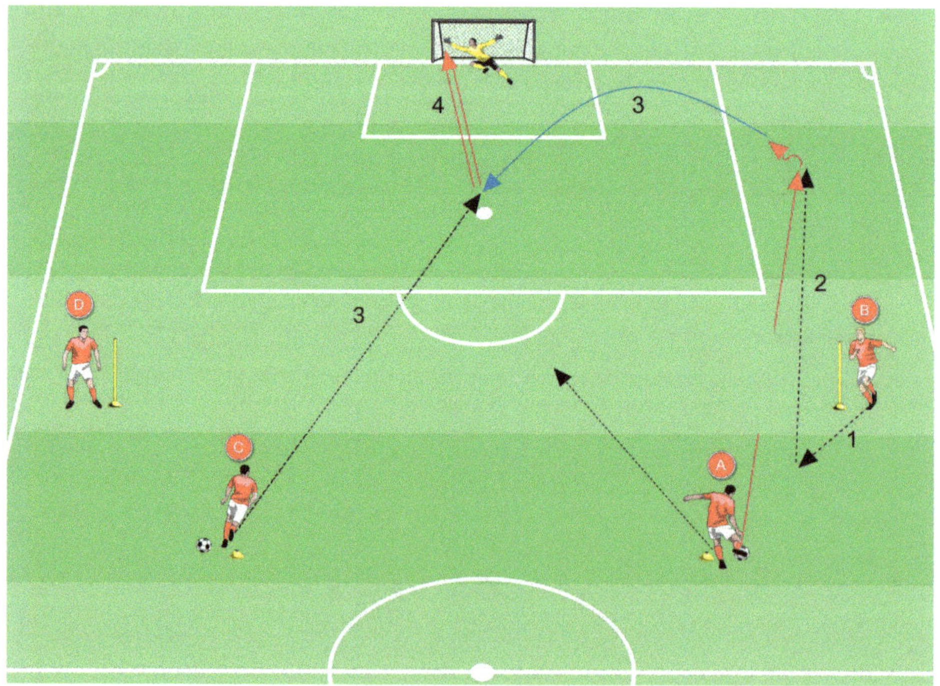

VARIATIONS

1.   Add on player D to finish off the delivered ball.

TRAINER'S TIPS

- Assure that the execution times of the loss of the marker must be carried out with maximum intensity.
- In a game play situation when the full back is beaten with a pass into space, the central defender will incorporate themself breaking the defensive line and creating space to incorporate another player. This situation demands a swap of markers by the defenders that, if not carried out in the right moment, can be very dangerous due to it happening in the final third.

LOSS OF MARKER, INCORPORATION AND SHOT ON GOAL

15

DURATION

10 minutes

OBJECTIVES

- Loss of marker in support
- Finishing
- Shot on goal
- Cut
- Incorporation
- Pass to the opening

MATERIALS

- 4 sticks
- Cones
- 1 goal
- Balls

PREPARATION

- Area of play: 50×50 meters
- Players: 8 + 1 goalkeeper
- Number of sets: 1 of 10 minutes

ORGANIZATION

At 30 meters from goal make a line of four sticks at 10 meters between each one, simulating a positioned defense. Player B sets up in the line of defense of the four sticks, while group A begins from the start cone, each player with a ball. The goalkeeper defends the goal.

DESCRIPTION

- B loses their marker heading towards teammate A.
- B changes direction heading to attack the depth between the sticks to receive the pass in space from A who will deliver it depending on the movement of B
- B finishes on net.
- At the end of the drill, A takes the spot of B while B, after having regained the ball, goes to the back of group A.

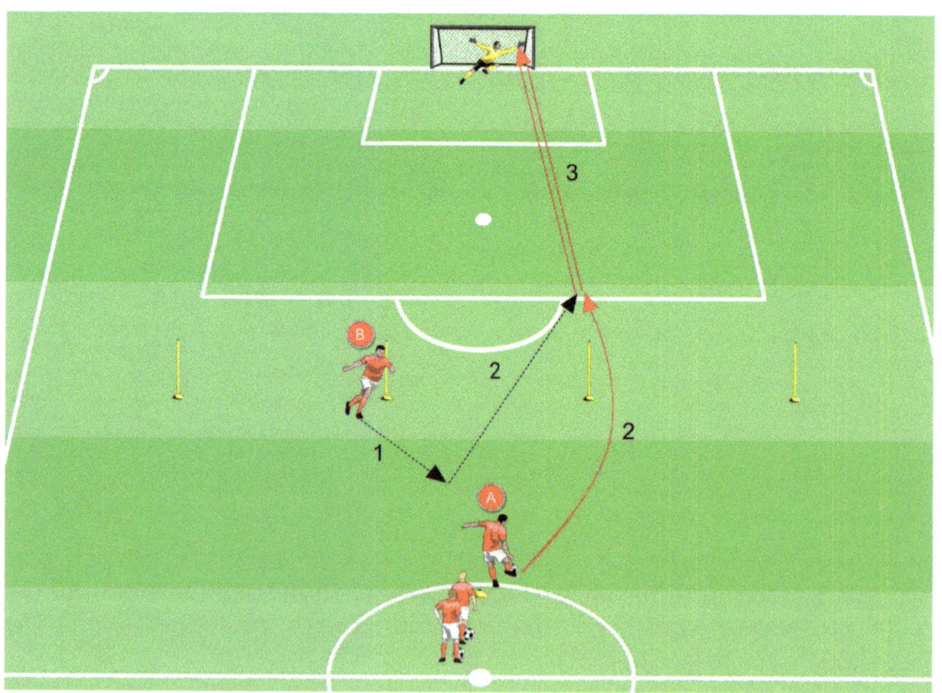

VARIATIONS

1. Shot on the first touch or maximum of two touches after the incorporation.
2. Add a defender passively marking the striker.

TRAINER'S TIPS

- This movement of losing the marker allows one to attack the space behind the defensive line.
- In a game situation, the defender tends to follow the first movement in approximation to not allow the striker to be able to turn.
- The player who passes the ball has to pay particular attention to the movement of their teammate, because the pass could be intercepted if not.

LOSING MARKER TO ATTRACT THE DEFENDER

16

HOW IT'S DONE — Simplified situation

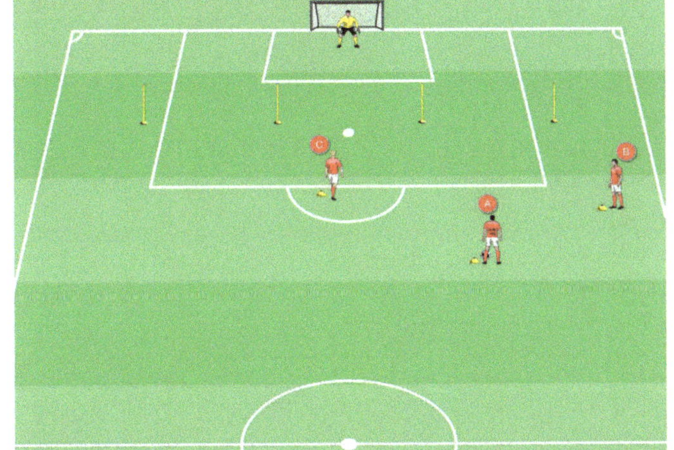

DURATION

14 minutes

OBJECTIVES

- Lose marker in support
- Movement to lose marker
- Ball in the area

MATERIALS

- 4 sticks
- 3 cones
- 1 goal
- Balls

PREPARATION

- Area of play: 50×40 meters
- Players: 10 + 1 goalkeeper
- Number of sets: 2 of 6 minutes 1 minute rest between the sets

ORGANIZATION

At 8 meters from the net place a line of four sticks, simulating a positioned defense. Players A, B and C set up alongside their cones to begin (like in the graphic). Put three players at each station. The goalkeeper tends to the goal.

DESCRIPTION

- B loses their marker going towards teammate A.
- B attacks the depth towards the outside to receive the pass in space from A, while C loses their marker at a slower speed going towards B.
- C changes direction attacking towards goal to receive the aerial delivery from B.
- C finishes on goal first touch.
- Upon the end of the drill A takes the spot of B, B takes that of C and C goes to the spot of A. Carry out the drill down the other side on the next rep.

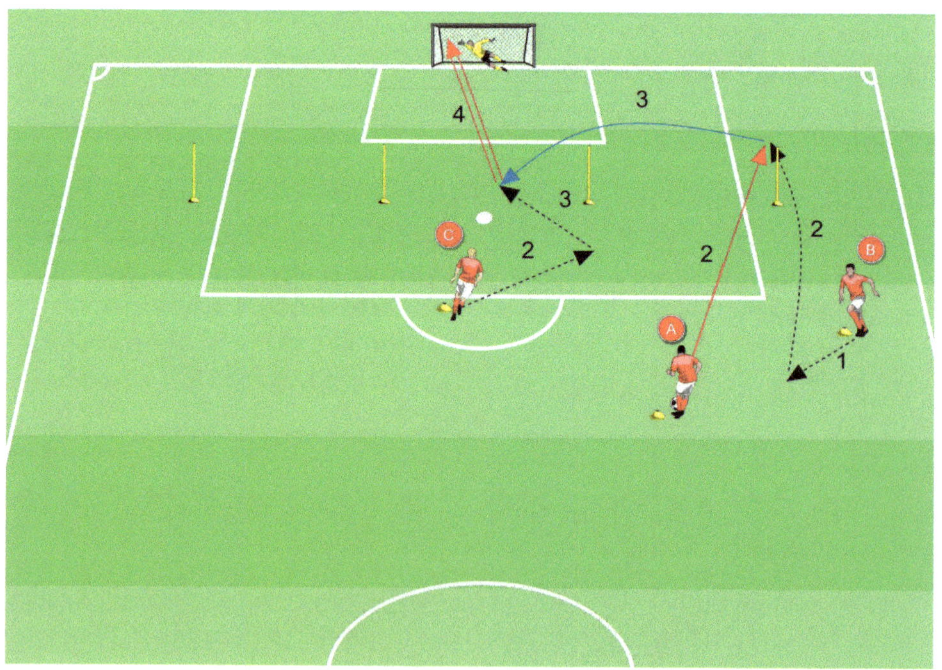

VARIATIONS

1. Add a passive defender who marks the striker that finishes on goal.

TRAINER'S TIPS

- This movement to lose the marker allows to win some time and space to get a shot in on goal.
- The player who swings the ball in has to pay particular attention to the movement of their teammate, to avoid an interception by the defense. They have to predict when their teammate will move in to finish it off, after sending the defender from one side to another.

COMING SHORT, DUMP OFF AND CUT

17

HOW IT'S DONE	Simplified situation

DURATION

12 minutes

OBJECTIVES

- Cut
- Support
- Penetration

MATERIALS

- 11 sticks
- 2 cones
- 1 pinny
- Balls

PREPARATION

- Area of play: 20×10 meters
- Players: 6
- Number of sets: 2 of 5 minutes with 1 minute break between sets

ORGANIZATION

Position the start cones in a line where we put A and B 10 meters apart between one another; in the middle put three sticks in a line so they create two fairly wide spaces to make a pass; in the same line as every start cone, make two goals with the sticks out wide. The defender C puts themself in line with the three sticks.

DESCRIPTION

- B comes to A anticipating C.
- A passes the ball to B.
- B gives the ball back to A.
- C will choose which space to occupy, where B loses the marker to the opposite side to receive the pass from A.
- B finishes on goal.

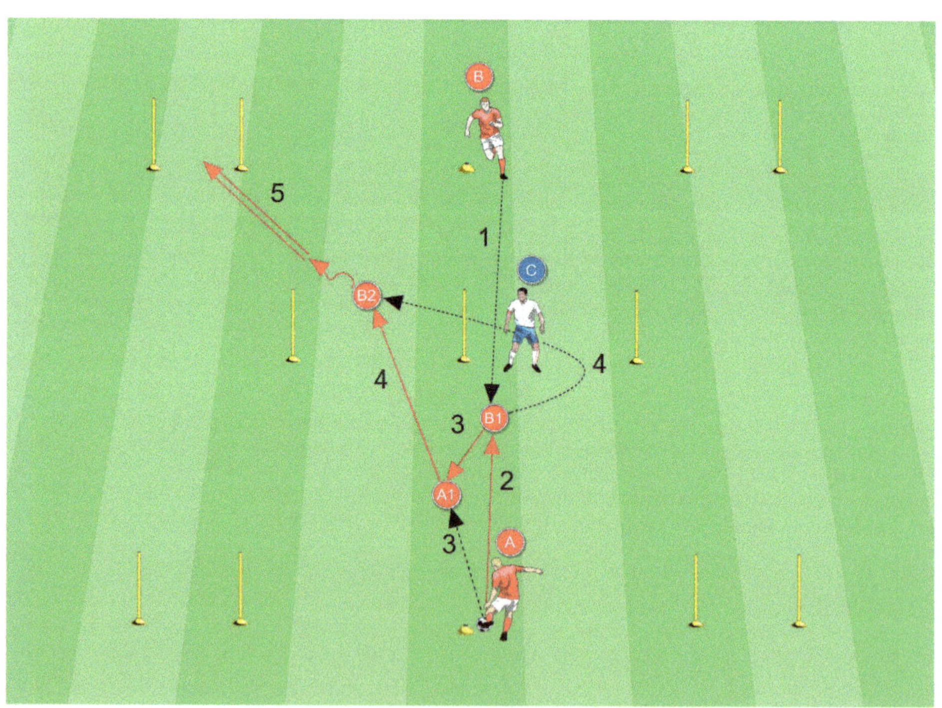

VARIATIONS

1. Defender C is activated to try and cut off the pass into space by A.
2. Defender C can track the unmarking by B to try and stay with him.

TRAINER'S TIPS

- Keep your eye on the body shape of C who has to watch to see if it will be A, passing the ball or B, who comes close to receive it.
- The dump off from B should be played using the outside foot.
- The pass from A towards the run by B, after having given it off, has to be well measured.
- Watch the shape of B which, after making the pass, should be set up so that they see the space in which they need to attack, without ever losing sight of either of the two.

LOSING MARKER, SWAP AND SHOT ON GOAL

18

HOW IT'S DONE — Simplified situation

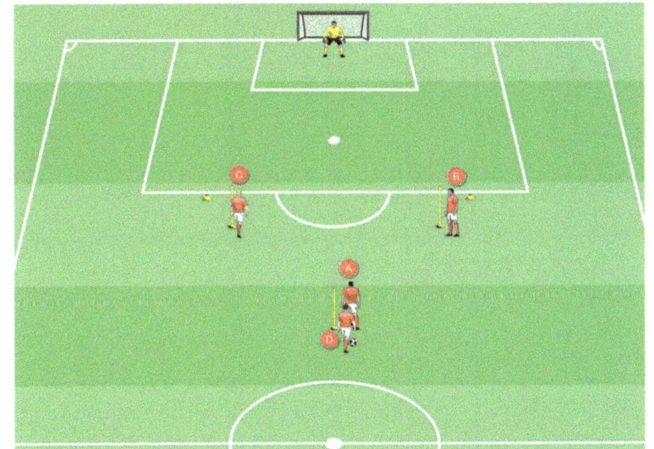

DURATION

15 minutes

OBJETIVOS

- Marker loss to come help
- Finishing
- Shot on goal
- Help
- Go back
- Cut
- Incorporation
- Pass into pass

MATERIALS

- 3 sticks
- 2 cones
- 1 goal
- Balls

PREPARATION

- Area of play: 50×40 meters
- Players: 8 + 1 goalkeeper
- Number of sets: 3 of 4 minutes with 1 minute of rest between sets

ORGANIZATION

Create a triangle with three sticks, two of which are close to the goal and 15 meters apart between them. Put between the two tall sticks, within a few meters, a diagonal of cones so the players have a way to lose their marker. Players A, B and C each position themselves next to a stick. Player A starts with the ball. The goal keeper protects the net. At each station indicated by a letter, place two players.

DESCRIPTION

- B loses their marker heading out wide (from stick to cone).
- A passes the ball to teammate B who comes close.
- B makes a pass returning the ball to A who comes close.
- B, in a circular run, attacks the depth losing their marker behind the stick to receive the pass in space from A.
- B finishes on goal.
- At the end of the move, A and B switch positions while players D and C carry out the same drill on the opposite side.

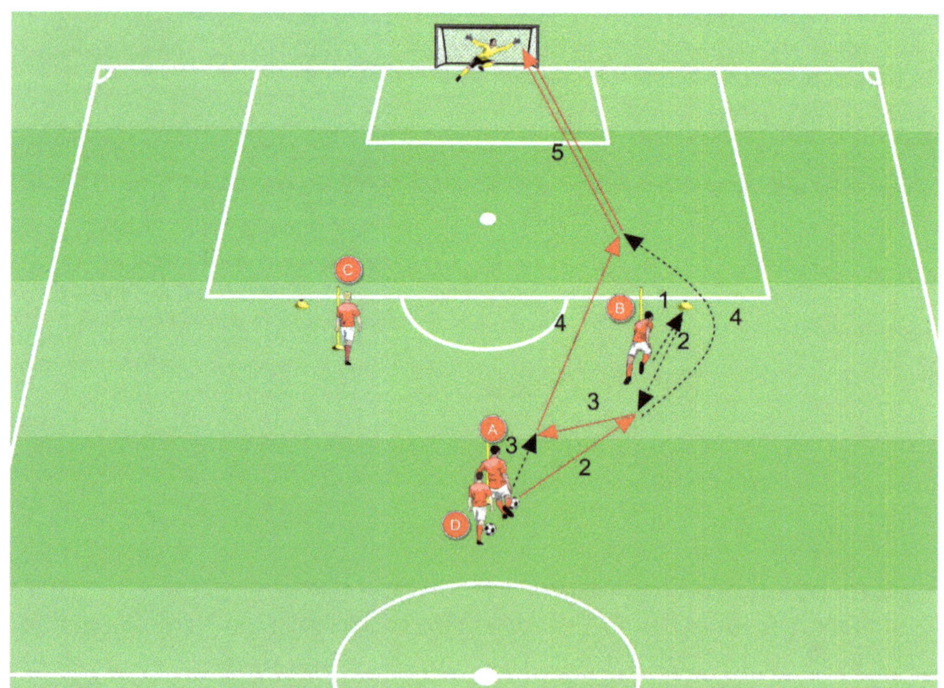

TRAINER'S TIPS

- For this type of movement it is necessary to pay particular attention to the shape and run of the player who will go to shoot.
- The last one carries out a movement in close to later on open themself up, showing their back to goal and never turning away from the ball.
- Attack the depth after having created width.

SEARCH FOR THE STRIKER, DUMP OFF AND INCORPORATION OF THE WINGERS

19

HOW IT'S DONE — **Simplified situation**

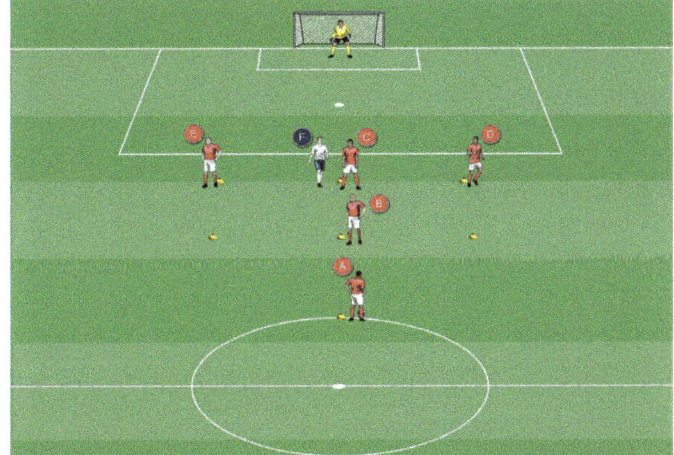

DURATION

20 minutes

OBJECTIVES

- **Incorporation**
- **Support**
- **Cut**

MATERIALS

- **7 cones**
- **1 pinny**
- **1 goal**
- **Balls**

PREPARATION

- **Area of play: 40×40 meters**
- **Playerss: 11 + 1 goalkeeper**
- **Number of sets: 2 of 9 minutes with one minute of rest between sets**

ORGANIZATION

Make two lines of three cones in each, the first one being 20 meters from goal and the second at 28 meters. C, D, E and defender F position themselves in the first line, B in the second and A begins from the start cone with a ball. The goalkeeper hangs in net. At each red station in the figure above, position two players.

DESCRIPTION

- B loses their marker deciding to go either to the left or to the right in regards to the vertical with A.
- C makes the opposite move of B.
- A passes the ball to striker C who dumps it off to B.
- B makes a pass into space down the wing (D or E) in the space left open by F who at the same time has chosen one of the two outside defenders to go and defend.
- The winger who receives the ball (E in the figure) finishes on goal.

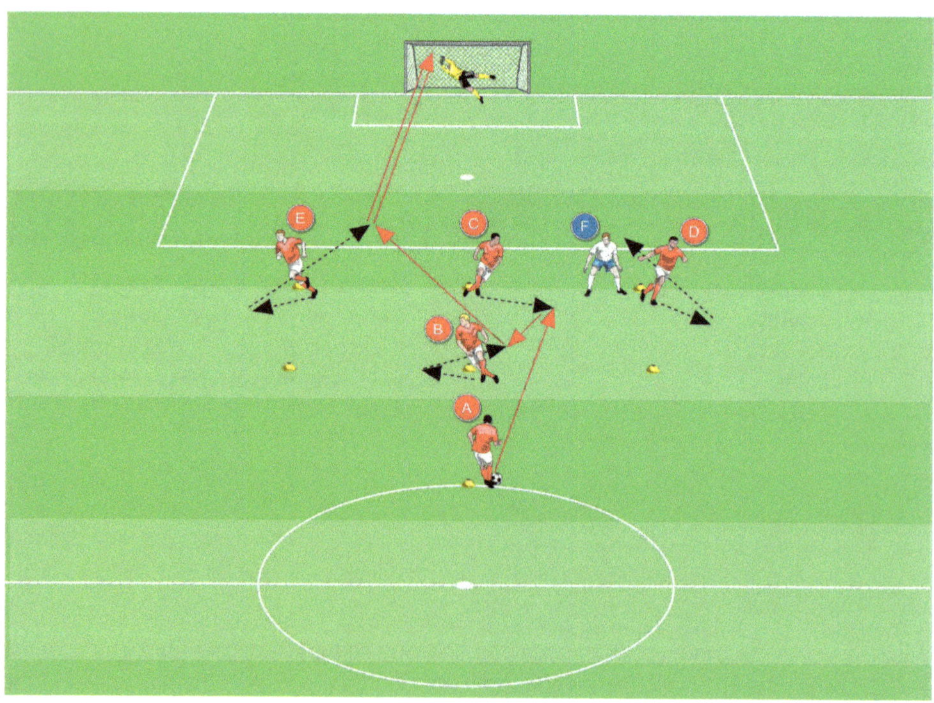

TRAINER'S TIPS

- So that C and B can receive it, they have to send their markers the wrong way with good timing.
- Once that is done, B dumps it off to C. Depending on where F finds themself, player D makes a pass into space towards one of the two wingers.
- B, after seeing which area F is guarding, will improve their peripheral vision.
- Verifying the timing of losing the markers in depth, paying special attention so that the players do not fall offside.

SEARCH FOR THE STRIKER, DUMP OFF AND INCORPORATION OF THE CENTRAL MIDFIELDER

20

HOW IT'S DONE · Simplified situation

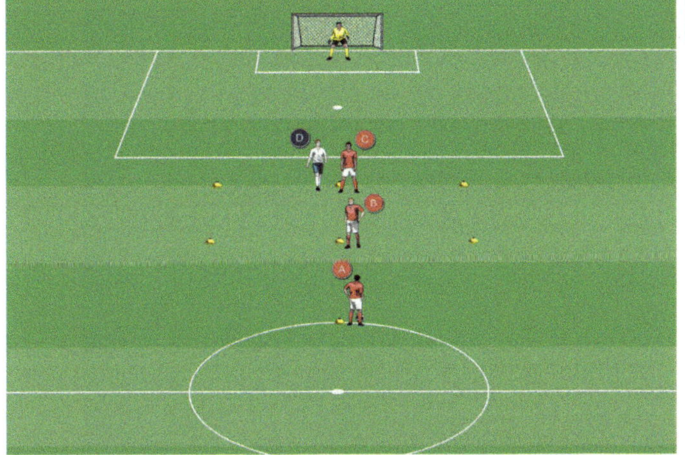

DURATION

20 minutes

OBJECTIVES

- Incorporation
- Help
- Pass into space

MATERIALS	PREPARATION
- 7 cones - 1 pinny - 1 goal - Balls	- Area of play: 40×40 meters - Players: 10 + 1 goalkeeper - Number of sets: 2 of 9 minutes with 1 minute of rest between sets

ORGANIZATION

Make two rows with three cones in each, the first being 20 meters from goal and the second being 28 meters away. C and D (this last one with a pinny) set up in the first row, B in the second and A begins at the start cone with the ball. The goalkeeper protects the net. Put two players at each red station.

DESCRIPTION

- B loses their marker choosing to either move left or right in regards to A.
- C goes in the opposite direction of B.
- A passes to C who also makes a pass.
- B works on his vision of play, finding the space occupied by defender D and decides to make the long pass into space or in deep towards A.
- A finishes on goal.

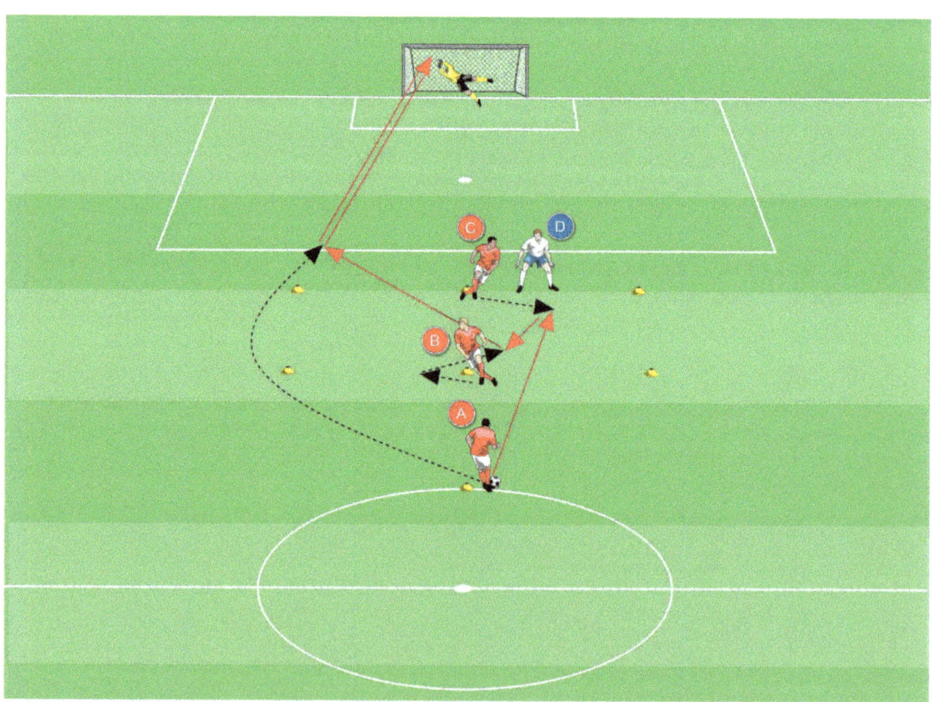

TRAINER'S TIPS

- Verify the timing of marker losses by B and C, that have to be in sync with their opposite direction movements.
- Work on the timing of the incorporation of A, that do not need to happen with a ton of anticipating so that it does not end in an offside.
- Work on the peripheral vision of B, who makes the pass into space.

BALL POSSESSION, FULLBACK INCORPORATION AND 1 ON 1

21

HOW IT'S DONE **Simplified situation**

DURATION

20 minutes

OBJECTIVES

- **Incorporation**
- **2 on 2**
- **Marker loss to come help**

MATERIALS

- 4 cones
- 2 sticks
- 6 pinnies
- 1 goal
- Balls

PREPARATION

- **Area of play: 50×50 meters**
- **Players: 12 + 1 goalkeeper**
- **Number of sets: 2 of 9 minutes with one minute rest between sets**

ORGANIZATION

At 20 meters from goal, create a square of 20×20 meters with the help of the cones. In the same row as the first two cones, place two sticks to indicate the outside areas. Inside the square, four players with a pinny and four more without set themselves up. Alongside the two outside posts go two players (one with a pinny and one without). The goalkeeper defends the net.

DESCRIPTION

- On the inside of the square defined by the cones, a 4 on 4 possession battle is played.
- When one of the teams manages to carry out five passes in a row, the player with the ball can leave freely from the square and take the ball to one of the two outside areas.
- In that moment the outside teammate makes a short-long cut to lose his marker to later receive the pass in-depth.
- One red player and one white one leave the square heading towards the net: the player of the team in possession has the goal as the objective while the other plays as a defender.

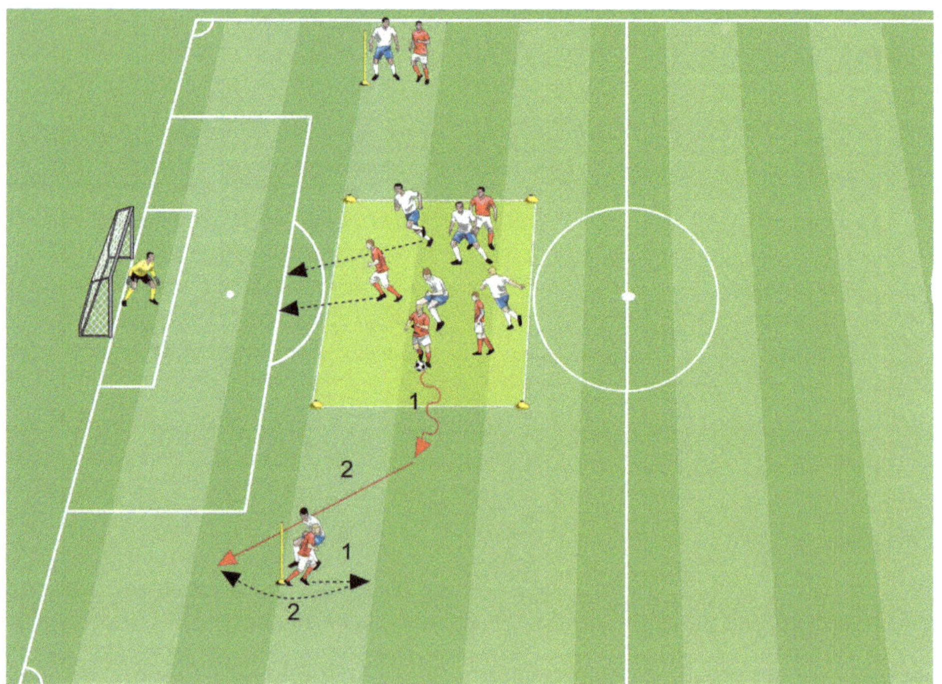

RULES

- When in possession of the ball, only two touches are allowed on the inside of the square.
- After five consecutive passes, the player with the ball can leave the square and the opponents cannot give chase. Only one red player and one white one can leave the square towards net.

TRAINER'S TIPS

- Work on the timing and the losing of the markers by the wingers.
- Encourage the battle in the center of the area, verifying the marker losing movements of the player who has to score as their objective.

BALL POSSESSION, WIDTH AND 2 ON 2

22

HOW IT'S DONE — Simplified situation

DURATION

20 minutes

OBJECTIVES

- Width
- 2 on 2
- Cut

MATERIALS

- 4 cones
- 2 sticks
- 6 pinnies
- 1 net
- Balls

PREPARATION

- Area of play: 50×50 meters
- Players: 12 + 1 goalkeeper
- Number of sets: 2 of 9 minutes with 1 minute of rest between sets

ORGANIZATION

20 meters from net, make a 20×20 meter square with the cones. On the same line as the first two cones, place two sticks to indicate the outer zones. Put four players with pinnies and four more without inside the square. Two players go on the side with the outer sticks (one with a pinny and another without). The goalkeeper protects the net.

DESCRIPTION

- A 4 on 4 ball possession game is carried out inside the square.
- When one of the two teams manages to make 5 consecutive passes, the player in possession can leave freely from the square with the ball towards one of the two outer wings.
- In that moment, the outside player will do a short-long move to ditch their marker to later receive the pass in deep with the opponent who could match them.
- At the same time, one white and red player head in towards the net: the player of the team in possession has the goal as their objective while the other plays in defense.
- The red players will have to move in to finish.

RULES

- There is a maximum of two touches inside the square.
- After five consecutive passes, the player with the ball can leave the square and the opponents can not give chase. Only one red player and one white one may leave from the square towards the net.

TRAINER'S TIPS

- After five consecutive passes, the player in possession leaves the square and breaks to the outside, who has to lose their marker with an in-out move to be able to create width.
- Once they receive the ball, two players (one of each team) enter the finishing zone and begin the 2 on 2 that will finish things out .

CHAPTER 3
ATTENTION TO DETAIL

4 - DRILLS TO RECEIVE DEPENDING ON THE SPACE AND THE OPPONENT

There are players who lose their markers so well that they do not have the need to protect the ball. With an ideal marker loss, that takes us to a good distance from the opponent and utilizing all the available space on the field, you can reduce the speed of the technique of the reception and carry it out with maximum attention.

What counts in the reception is the direction, which can change the feel of the move, means it is best to receive with the foot that is furthest from the opponent to protect the ball.

But how much space do we have on hand? How far away do we find the opponent? If we are familiar with the space and time on hand, we can decide how to make the reception.

The player that has to receive the ball has to know what to do with it before getting it, but has to decide that depending on the situation and

decide before it comes. Working the orientated reception, based on the position of the opponent, gives more fluidity to play and obviously allows us to not lose the ball.

Reaction times, depending on the spaces at hand, must be trained and can be improved utilizing situations of play, analytically correcting, or giving simple indications of possible solutions to the players. A simple sign of *pressing,* passive first and then active, permits the players to learn at first without the pressure of the opponent but recognizing that they will be there, keeping calm about possible solutions and escapes, to later on try out the difference in a game play situation, where the opponent has the chance to take away the ball.

CLOSED OR OPEN RECEPTION

23

HOW IT'S DONE	Simplified situation

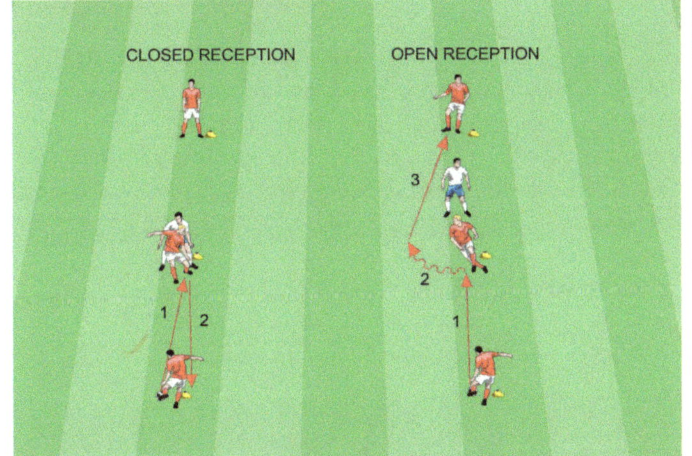

DURATION

10 minutes

OBJECTIVES

- Orientated control to open
- Orientated control to close

MATERIALS

- 3 cones
- 1 pinny
- Balls

PREPARATION

- Area of play: 20×10 meters
- Players: 4
- Number of sets: 4 of 2 minutes with 30 seconds of rest between sets

ORGANIZATION

Place 3 cones vertically at 8 meters between each other. At the middle cone there should be two players (one with a pinny and another without), while two players go at the other cones without pinnies.

DESCRIPTION

- Closed reception: the player without a pinny in the middle comes close to receive the pass from the teammate. They are followed by their marker with a pinny and, as a result, the player without a pinny carries out a closed reception protecting the ball and handing it off again to their teammate.
- Open reception: the player without the pinny in the middle comes close to get the pass from his teammate. The defender with the pinny waits and, therefore, the player without one makes an open reception and goes to find their teammate on the other side.
- Substitute the pairing in the middle at the beginning of each set.

RULES

- The red players play with a maximum of two touches.

TRAINER'S TIPS

- It is important to work on the body shape of the players who are making the reception.
- The player that gets it has to position themself in a way so that they can see the ball and the possible opponent.
- Depending on the choice of attacking or waiting for the opposition, one can decide to protect or leave the ball uncovered.

BEAT THE OPPONENT WITH A RECEPTION

24

HOW IT'S DONE — Simplified situation

DURATION

15 minutes

OBJECTIVES

- Orientated control to open
- Reaction
- Peripheral vision

MATERIALS

- 8 cones
- Balls

PREPARATION

- Area of play: 10×10 meters
- Players: 8
- Number of sets: 3 of 4 minutes with one minute rest between sets

ORGANIZATION

Create a 10×10 meter square that has another on the inside that is 5×5 meters with the cones. The players set up like in the figure above.

DESCRIPTION

- The drill includes a continuous sequence of passes along the perimeter of the outside square.
- To begin the sequence, it can start from any point.
- A passes to B.
- During the pass, C starts from the cone and passively presses B.
- B will decide which direction to go with the first reception depending on the space that C occupies and once beaten C with a touch passes to D or returns it to A.
- C and B quickly swap positions .
- The drill is the same for the whole series .

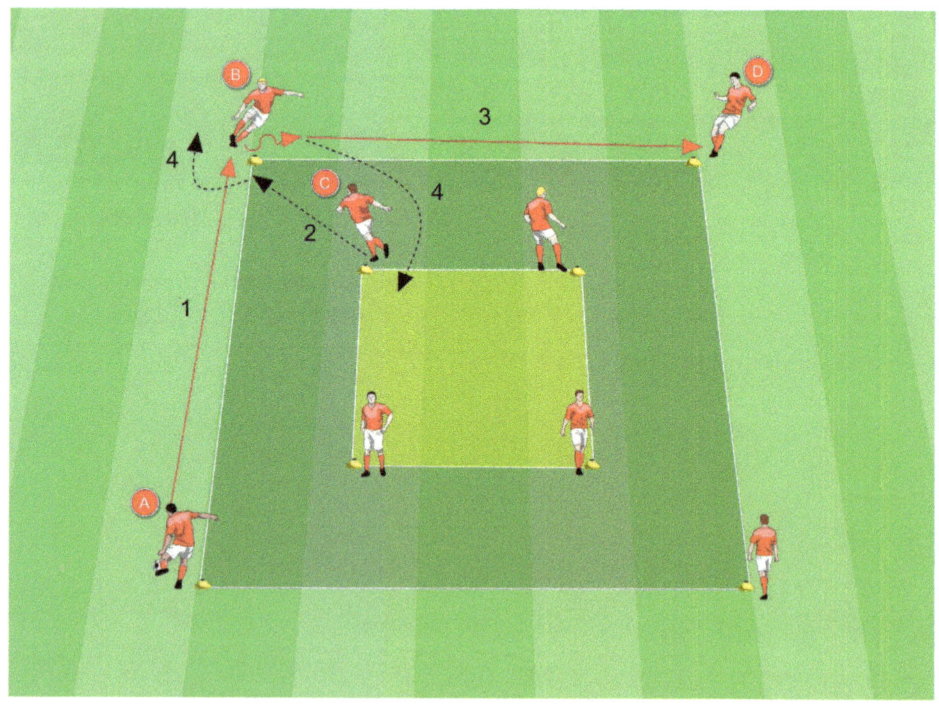

RULES

- The outside players have a maximum of two touches: they choose the direction on the first and pass it off to a teammate with the second.

TRAINER'S TIPS

- The player that receives the ball works on the orientated control technique and reaction times, depending on which side the defender presses from in front of them.
- This way, the player who receives it works on their peripheral vision and concentrates more on the open space to attack.

ORIENTATED CONTROL IN THE SPACE CREATED BY TEAMMATES

25

HOW IT'S DONE — Simplified situation

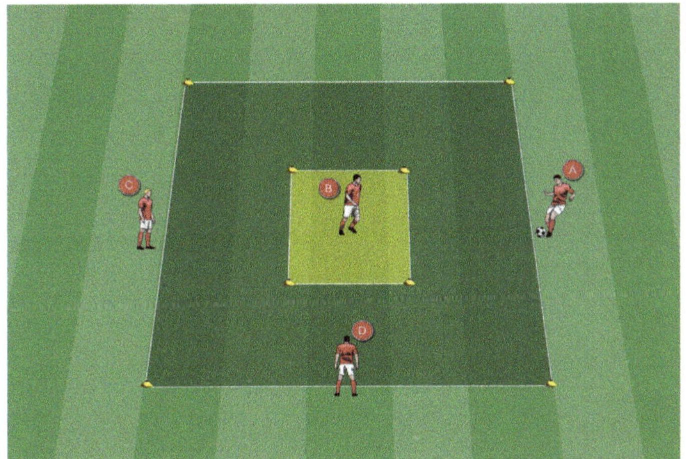

DURATION

15 minutes

OBJECTIVES

- Orientated control
- Reaction
- Peripheral vision

MATERIAL

- 8 cones
- Balls

PREPARATION

- Area of play: 20×20 meters
- Players: 4
- Number of sets: 3 of 4 minutes with one minute of rest between sets

ORGANIZATION

Create a square of 20×20 meters with the cones; players A, B and C take three sides with the final side open. Make a little square inside the big one of 8×8 meters where player B sets up in the middle.

DESCRIPTION

- A passes the ball to B who finds himself in the little square.
- A moves to the free side.
- C and D move based on the movement of A, while B with an orientated control pushes the ball towards the open side left by the three teammates.
- The drill is continuous during the entire set.

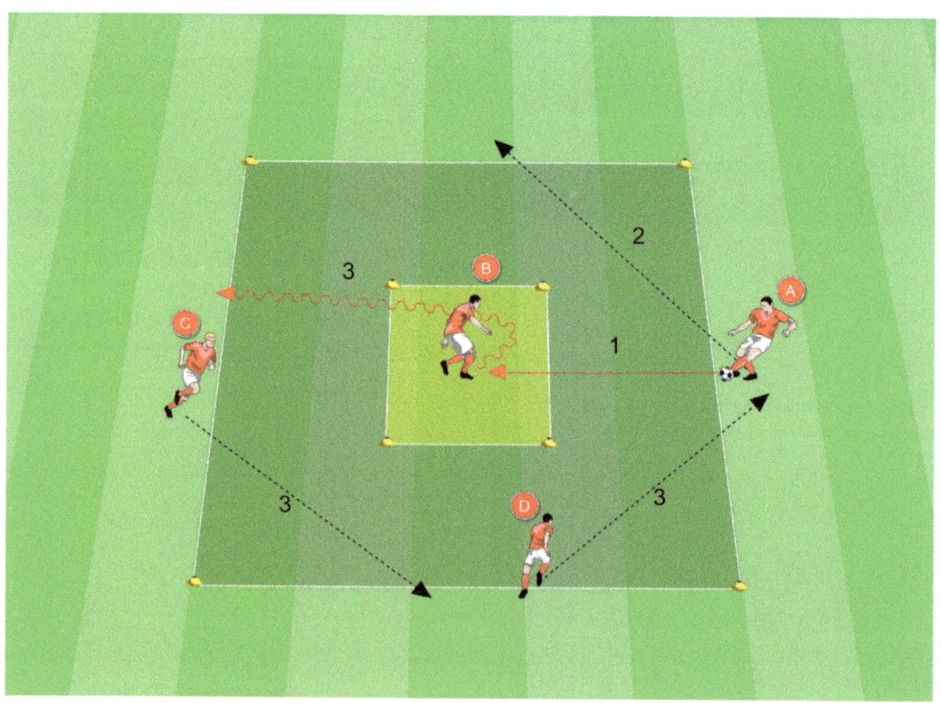

RULES

- The player that receives the ball in the inside square has just one touch (orientated control) to be able to leave the square. The player that passes the ball (A, in the figure) determines the movement of the teammates who will have to leave a side open that the teammate will occupy (B, in the figure).

TRAINER'S TIPS

- The player who gets it on the inside of the small square, with an orientated reception, has to leave the square.
- The side where they drive the ball to is the one the teammates have left open, working on reaction time and peripheral vision.
- The player that passes the ball to the inside, decides to go clockwise or counter clockwise, while the others on the outside move accordingly.

ATTACK AGAINST DEFENSE: 5 VS WITH FINISHING ZONE

26

HOW IT'S DONE — Simplified situation

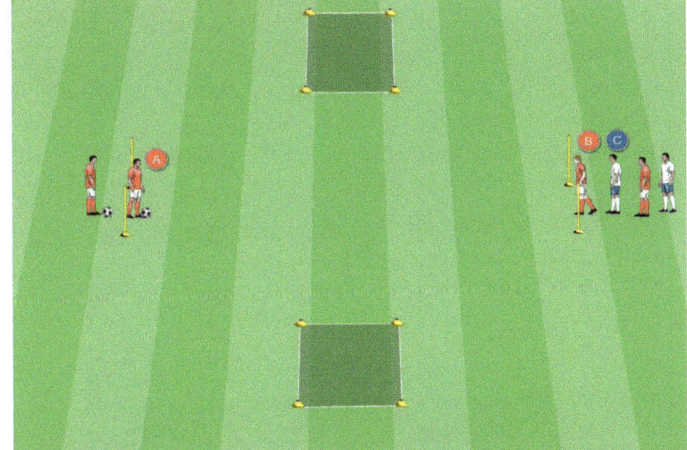

DURATION

20 minutes

OBJECTIVES

- Orientated control
- 2 on 1

MATERIALS

- 4 sticks
- 8 cones
- Balls
- 2 pinnies

PREPARATION

- Area of play: 20×15 meters
- Players: 6
- Number of sets: 4 of 4 minutes with 1 minute of rest between sets

ORGANIZATION

Place two goals of 2.5 meters in front of one another 15 meters apart. At midfield level of the field of play, positioned out wide, create two squares of 5×5 meters (like in the figure). The players of group A have one ball each and start in net, while in the other net players B and C start, this last one with a pinny.

DESCRIPTION

- B sprints towards the inside to one of the inside empty squares.
- A gives them the ball, while C (defender) decides whether to anticipate, press or await the movement of B.
- B, depending on the choice of C, will make an open or closed reception and once B touches the ball, the 2 on 1 starts (A and B with C).
- A and B have to score on goal where B started, while if C regains the ball, they can go score in the other net.

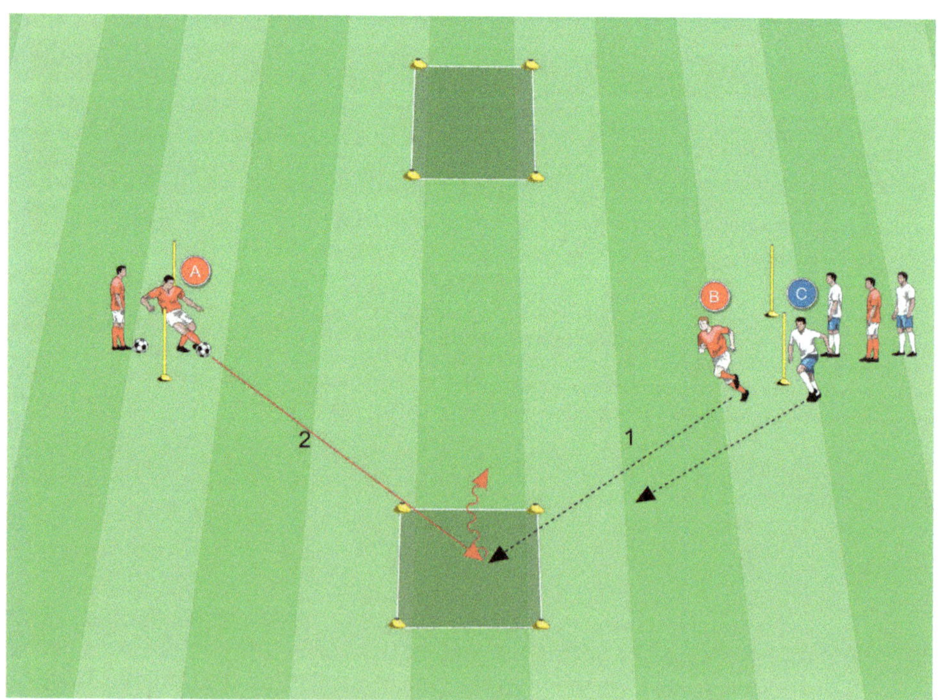

RULES

- A and B during the 2 on 1 have a maximum of three touches.
- Defender C, if they regain the ball, has unlimited touches to go score on the mini net.

TRAINER'S TIPS

- B starts with a move to possibly lose their marker, attacking a square. C will choose to anticipate them, attack them so they cannot turn, or wait and protect the net.
- B, depending on the choice of C, will have to go close to avoid anticipating and make an open or closed reception.
- When B receives the ball, A makes the unload and can start the 2 on 1.

CONCLUSIONS

The search for space represents the necessary base to train the players to move themselves continuously, to receive and attack the depth.

Keeping the ball on the ground is not enough: to have a good possession of the ball, it is necessary to work the concept of losing their marker, because if not, the player with the ball will not have the proper options. Possession of the ball is also not sufficient: it helps to have more chances to create danger, but if not managed, will not do you much. When the moment to attack arrives, it is necessary to incorporate all the spaces, particularly with the teams that give them up. The player that attacks the space after losing their marker and the player that makes the pass have to have the same idea of play, same vision of play and make the same situational decision, with the help of the trainer who helps them work on the timing.

ABOUT THE AUTHOR

Matteo Von Der Horst
UEFA Trainer C

Matteo Von Der Horst (Capri 1992), of German and Spanish nationality, is a UEFA C trainer.

He began his journey as a trainer at 17 with Bassanello Guizza. Two years later he signed for Albignasego, where he trained various levels, to later fully focus on the Cadete category for 2 years. There he won the regional league championship.

He is currently the trainer of Centro Federal Italiano in Napoli.